P9-CQJ-255

ZOMBIES
AND OTHER WALKING DEAD

by Ruth Owen

Consultant: Troy Taylor
President of the American Ghost Society

BEARPORT
PUBLISHING

New York, New York

Credits

Cover and Title Page, ©isoga/Shutterstock and ©Andreas Gradin/Shutterstock; 4–5, ©Fer Gregory/Shutterstock; 5, ©redfrisbee/Shutterstock; 6–7, ©tandemich/Shutterstock; 7, ©Greg Daniels/Shutterstock; 9, ©Julie Dermansky/Corbis; 10L, ©Jamie Cross/Shutterstock; 10TR, ©Chad Zuber/Shutterstock; 10BR, ©Picsfive/Shutterstock; 11, ©Kim Jones; 12–13, ©Joloei/Shutterstock, ©Yuri Arcurs/Shutterstock, ©Greg Daniels/Shutterstock, ©CURA Photography/Shutterstock, and ©defpicture/Shutterstock; 14–15, ©Blend Images/Shutterstock, ©Cheryl Casey/Shutterstock, ©Daniel Korzeniewski/Shutterstock, and ©Henry Hazboun/Shutterstock; 16–17, ©Jean-Claude Francolon/Getty Images; 18T, ©Vilor/Shutterstock; 18B, ©Anest/Shutterstock; 19, ©Dave Fleetham/Corbis; 20–21, ©Kim Jones; 22–23, ©Sandra Cunningham/Shutterstock and ©Fer Gregory/Shutterstock; 24–25, ©Juhku/Shutterstock, ©Vladimir Sazonov/Shutterstock, ©Norimages/Alamy, and ©Pedro Rufo/Shutterstock; 26, ©Losevsky Photo and Video/Shutterstock; 27, ©andesign101/Shutterstock; 28L, ©Alice Mary Herden Green-Fly Media LLC/Shutterstock, ©sgame/Shutterstock, and ©Kim Jones; 29L, ©Jeff Thrower/Shutterstock; 29R, ©Chris Harvey/Shutterstock and ©fuyu liu/Shutterstock.

Publisher: Kenn Goin
Senior Editor: Joyce Tavolacci
Creative Director: Spencer Brinker
Design: Emma Randall
Editor: Mark J. Sachner
Photo Researcher: Ruby Tuesday Books Ltd

Library of Congress Cataloging-in-Publication Data
Owen, Ruth, 1967-
  Zombies and other walking dead / by Ruth Owen.
    p. cm. — (Not near normal: the paranormal)
  Includes bibliographical references and index.
  ISBN-13: 978-1-61772-721-4 (library binding)
  ISBN-10: 1-61772-721-0 (library binding)
  1. Zombies—Juvenile literature. I. Title.
  GR581.094 2013
  398.21—dc23
                              2012039500

Copyright © 2013 Bearport Publishing Company, Inc. All rights reserved. No part of this publication may be reproduced in whole or in part, stored in any retrieval system, or transmitted in any form or by any means, electronic, mechanical, photocopying, recording, or otherwise, without written permission from the publisher.

For more information, write to Bearport Publishing Company, Inc., 45 West 21st Street, Suite 3B, New York, New York 10010. Printed in the United States of America.

10 9 8 7 6 5 4 3 2

Contents

The Strange Case of Felicia Felix-Mentor

One morning in October 1936, a strange woman appeared in Ennery, a village in Haiti. The woman's clothes were torn. Her skin was pale gray and cracked. She covered her eyes with a dark rag to keep out the bright sunlight. The woman could barely speak and seemed confused as she walked around aimlessly.

Crowds of people gathered to see the strange woman. One group of villagers, the Mentor family, believed they recognized her. They said she was Felicia Felix-Mentor, a family member who had died and been buried in 1907—almost 30 years before! Now it appeared that Felicia was back from the dead. According to the villagers, there could be only one explanation—Felicia had been turned into a **zombie**.

Was the strange woman who appeared in Ennery, Haiti, really Felicia Felix-Mentor back from the dead?

An Important Clue?

At the time of her death, Felicia Felix-Mentor had limped because she had once broken her left leg. The zombie-like Felicia, who appeared many years later, also had trouble walking.

Back from the Dead?

Is it possible for a dead person to be brought back to life as a zombie? Was the mysterious woman Felicia Felix-Mentor? To find out, a team of doctors carefully examined her.

They soon discovered that the woman had difficulty walking because she was weak from hunger—not because of an old leg injury. Also, she was wandering alone and confused because she was **mentally ill**. The woman was not Felicia Felix-Mentor after all, and she was definitely not a zombie! So why did the Mentor family and other villagers think she was a zombie?

Meeting a Zombie

In the 1920s, an American writer and explorer named William Seabrook visited Haiti. Seabrook said that during his visit, he had seen zombies. He described the creatures as walking in a slow, plodding way with empty, staring eyes.

Voodoo and Zombies

In Haiti, people have believed in the existence of zombies for hundreds of years. This belief comes from a religion called **voodoo** that can be traced back to Africa.

In the 1500s, Europeans began capturing Africans and taking them to North and South America where they were forced into **slavery**. Some enslaved Africans were brought to work on **plantations** in Haiti. Many of them continued to believe in and practice voodoo.

According to Haitian tales, zombies are created by a certain kind of voodoo **witch doctor**, or priest. Most witch doctors are healers who help sick people and perform religious ceremonies. However, a small number of witch doctors called **bokors** are believed to be evil and harm people.

Bokors are said to have magical powers, which they use to do terrible things. One of the most horrifying things they do is raise dead bodies from their **graves** and turn them into zombies.

Items used by a voodoo priest in religious ceremonies

Voodoo Body Snatchers

For hundreds of years, people in Haiti have been terrified of coming back from the dead as zombies. To stop a voodoo bokor from stealing their dead bodies, some people ask for the doors to their **tombs** to be locked after they die.

United States

Atlantic Ocean

Haiti

Mexico

Caribbean Sea

Pacific Ocean

SOUTH AMERICA

N W E S

Making a Zombie

Why would a bokor want to turn another person into a zombie? Stories say that a bokor gets paid to kill a person and then bring his or her body back from the dead. The bokor might do this for someone who wants an enemy turned into a zombie. A bokor might also create a zombie to act as his or her own personal slave.

In voodoo **legends**, a bokor must first kill his or her victim to make a zombie. The bokor carries out this terrible act by putting a powerful, poisonous powder on the victim's skin. This zombie powder includes ingredients such as ground-up deadly **puffer fish**, toad skin, and human bones. Once the powder has killed the victim, the body is buried. Then the bokor digs up the corpse and casts a magic spell over it. This brings the dead body back to life as a zombie.

Zombie Cucumber

To keep a victim in a zombie-like state, a bokor regularly feeds the zombie a paste made from a poisonous plant known as zombie cucumber.

Ti Joseph's Zombies

One haunting tale from Haiti tells the story of a bokor named Ti Joseph. In 1918, Joseph is said to have turned nine dead men into zombies.

Joseph forced the men to work on a sugar cane plantation. Each week he collected the zombies' wages from the plantation owner and kept the money for himself.

One day, Joseph's wife felt sorry for the zombies and gave them some candy. Unfortunately for her husband, the candy contained salty nuts. According to legend, if a zombie eats salt, the bokor's spell is broken. After the zombies ate the candy, Joseph could no longer control them. The nine men immediately walked back to the graveyard, fell into their graves, and began to rot.

A Fate Worse Than Death

A powerful fear of being turned into a zombie slave has been a part of voodoo beliefs for hundreds of years. Much of this fear may come from the fact that the **ancestors** of many Haitians were forced into slavery. For many people, to be turned into a mindless zombie slave is a fate worse than death.

Clairvius Narcisse, Dead or Alive?

One of the most terrifying zombie stories involves a Haitian man named Clairvius Narcisse. On April 30, 1962, Clairvius had terrible stomach pains and was ice cold. He also struggled to breathe and move. So he went to a hospital in the town of Deschapelle, Haiti.

Not long after, on May 2, 1962, Clairvius died from the mysterious illness. His death was confirmed by two doctors. The next day, Clairvius's cold body was buried as his family watched and wept.

One day, 18 years later, Clairvius's sister, Angelina Narcisse, was at the market in the family's home village. Suddenly, she came face to face with a man who looked just like her dead brother. Had Clairvius come back from the dead?

The Real Clairvius Narcisse

The mysterious man was able to prove he was Clairvius by sharing his childhood nickname with his sister. Only close family members knew and used this name.

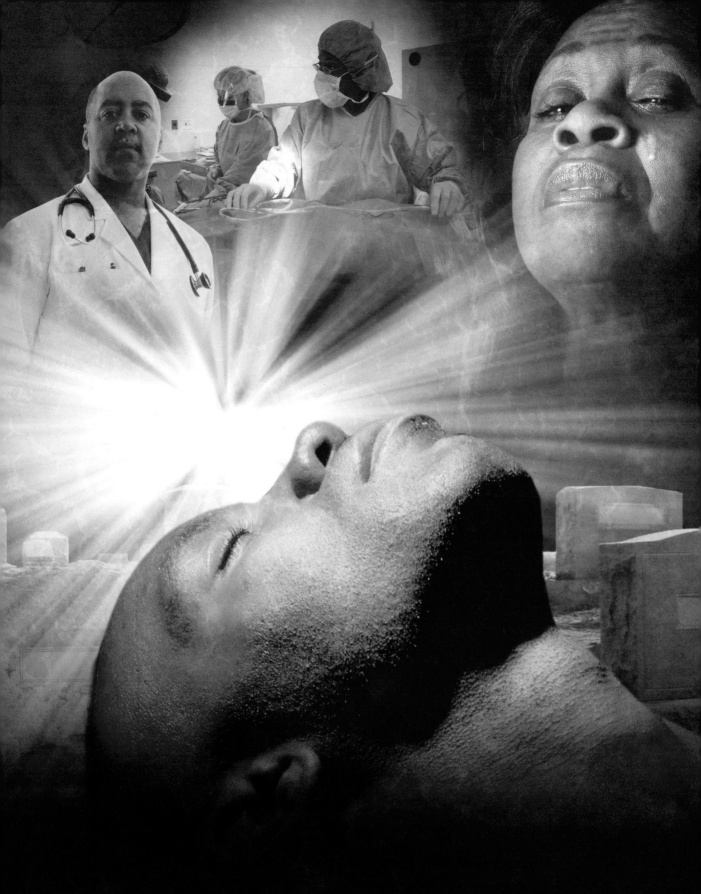

Brother Zombie

Clairvius Narcisse had an amazing story to tell. He told his sister, Angelina, that he remembered the doctors pronouncing him dead on May 2, 1962. At the time, Clairvius could not speak or move. He was somehow trapped inside his lifeless body, but he was still very much alive. Later, Clairvius remembered the sound of nails being pounded into his wooden **coffin**. Yet he was unable to scream for help. Then his coffin was lowered into a grave, and, to his horror, he was buried alive!

Clairvius did not know how long he was in his grave, but some time later, a bokor opened his coffin. According to Clairvius, the bokor forced him to work on a sugar plantation and fed him zombie cucumber paste. The paste caused Clairvius to fall into a dreamlike state. He believed he had become a zombie.

After two years, the bokor died. Clairvius was no longer made to eat the paste, and his zombie-like state wore off. He ran away from the plantation. For the next 16 years, Clairvius wandered the countryside before going back to his home village.

A Brother's Revenge

Before his terrible ordeal, Clairvius had argued with his brother over some family land that both men wanted. Clairvius believed that, in an act of revenge, his brother had paid the bokor to turn him into a zombie. Clairvius only returned home once he heard his brother had died.

This 1982 photo shows Clairvius Narcisse sitting on the grave where he was buried alive in May, 1962.

Zombie Science

Why did two doctors think Clairvius Narcisse was dead, when he was actually still alive? Some scientists think the answer lies in zombie powder. The poisonous powder made by bokors contains a deadly **neurotoxin** from the puffer fish. When the poison gets into a person's blood, it **paralyzes** the body. The person's heart nearly stops so that the heartbeat is hard to detect. Even a doctor may not be able to tell if the victim is dead or alive. However, once the poison's effects have worn off, the victim would appear to have miraculously come back to life.

Is this how bokors appear to kill people and then **resurrect** them? Is this what happened to Clairvius Narcisse? In the world of voodoo zombies, there are many mysteries left to be solved.

A datura flower

Not All Vegetables Are Good for You

The zombie cucumber plant is also called datura. A person made to eat poisonous datura flowers, fruits, or seeds would suffer confusion, fear, and memory loss. The confused victim might even believe that he or she has become a zombie.

A datura fruit, also known as a zombie cucumber

A porcupine puffer fish

Evil Revenants

Throughout history, horrifying stories of creatures coming back from the dead have been told around the world. In 1090, near the town of Burton-Upon-Trent, in England, it is said that walking corpses terrorized a small village.

The story tells of two men who died in the town and were then buried in a graveyard. Later that evening, however, the men suddenly reappeared in the village.

All night, the men walked around the village carrying their coffins on their shoulders. They shouted and banged on the walls of houses. The terrified villagers had heard many old legends of people returning from the dead. They believed the two men had become evil zombies called **revenants**.

Returning from the Dead

The word *revenant* comes from the **Latin** word *revenans*, which means "returning."

Getting Rid of Revenants

In old European tales, revenants climb out of their graves to harm the living by spreading disease. In the village near Burton-Upon-Trent, the story says that any villager who spoke to the two revenants soon became sick and died. The people knew that in order to save themselves, they had to stop the evil walking corpses.

The villagers waited until the revenants had climbed back into their graves. Then they dug up the two dead bodies. To be sure that the revenants would not return, the villagers chopped off the corpses' heads and cut out their hearts. The two revenants were never seen again.

Revenants: Fact or Fiction?

Did people really see revenants that had climbed from their graves? One possible explanation could be that in the past, people in **comas** might have been buried by mistake. If they woke up and were then able to escape from their graves, it would have looked as if they were returning from the dead.

Toxic Zombies

They moan and groan. They walk very slowly, smashing through doors or walls that stand in their way.

Skin peels from their rotting bodies. Sometimes an arm or other body part falls off, but that doesn't keep these monsters from looking for a bloody meal. These horrific creatures are called **toxic** zombies, and they are hungry for human brains and flesh!

Toxic zombies get their name because a disease or something poisonous, or toxic, has brought them back to life to terrorize the living. The only way to stop these zombies from hurting and killing people is to destroy their brains. Thankfully, toxic zombies only appear in horror movies and TV shows.

The First Toxic Zombies

Toxic zombies first appeared in a 1968 movie called *Night of the Living Dead*. In the movie, scientists think the dead bodies may be coming back to life because of **radiation** from a satellite that fell to Earth from space.

Zombies on the March

You cannot go forward or backward. All around you are groaning, openmouthed zombies with blank eyes. There's nowhere to escape! Don't be afraid, though, it's just a zombie walk.

Every year in cities around the world, thousands of people dress up as zombies and take part in a zombie walk, or march. Often, the zombies march to bring attention to an important issue, such as world hunger. They bring or collect gifts of food, which are then given to people in the city who do not have enough to eat.

So don't be alarmed if you see a tattered, horrific zombie looking for food. It's not going to eat your brains—it's just helping out your neighbors!

A zombie walk in Moscow, Russia.

A rotting zombie prowls the streets of Brisbane, Australia.

Zombie Record-Breakers

At the Mexico City zombie walk in 2011, a record-breaking 9,860 zombies turned out.

Zombies Around the World

Check out who's who in the world of zombies. What do zombies from around the world look like? How do they behave? Most importantly, find out how people can destroy these bloodthirsty creatures that refuse to stay dead.

Viking Draugr

Location: Northern Europe and parts of North America

Description: A Viking *draugr* has long hair and a beard and wears a metal helmet. Its large body possesses superhuman strength. Sometimes, the creature appears in the form of a cat.

Behavior: A *draugr* stays close to or inside its tomb, guarding the treasure it has collected during its life.

How to destroy: A hero must cut off the *draugr's* head and then jump between the head and the body before the two parts hit the ground!

Chinese Hopping Zombie

Location: China

Description: A Chinese hopping zombie has green mold growing on its skin. Its corpse is very stiff, so it cannot bend its legs to walk. Instead, it hops on two feet with stiff, outstretched arms. It may have died centuries before, so it may wear old-fashioned clothes.

Behavior: By day, this zombie hides in caves or in its grave. At night, it searches for people to kill so that it can take their life force.

How to escape: A person can distract the zombie by throwing some sticky rice on the ground. The zombie will have to stop hopping to count each rice grain, and then the person will have enough time to escape.

Revenant

Location: Throughout Europe but mostly in Great Britain

Description: A revenant looks like a pale, ghostly corpse. Its clothes may be muddy from climbing out of its grave.

Behavior: A revenant climbs from its grave at night and wanders around the village or town where it once lived, frightening family members, friends, and neighbors—and spreading disease.

How to destroy: When the creature is back in its grave, dig up the body. Then, chop off the revenant's head and cut out its heart. To be extra sure it is destroyed, burn all the pieces of the corpse.

Toxic Zombie

Location: Worldwide

Description: A toxic zombie's skin may be very pale or a greenish-blue color because its body is rotting. It may have missing limbs and maggots living in its empty eye sockets.

Behavior: A toxic zombie often spends time in a city where there are plenty of people to feed on. If a panicked person runs over it with a car or hits it with a heavy object, the zombie feels no pain and shows no distress.

How to destroy: With an axe or shovel, aim for the creature's head and try to destroy its brain.

Glossary

ancestors (AN-sess-turz) family members who lived a long time ago

bokors (BOH-kurz) voodoo priests or sorcerers who are believed to use their supernatural powers for evil purposes, such as creating zombies

coffin (KAWF-in) a long box in which a dead person is buried

comas (KOH-muhz) states in which a person is unconscious and cannot wake up; can be caused by drugs, disease, or injury

graves (GRAYVZ) holes dug into the ground where dead people are buried

Latin (LAT-uhn) a language spoken in ancient Rome

legends (LEJ-uhndz) stories handed down that may be based on fact but are not always completely true

mentally ill (MEN-tuhl-ee IL) having a brain that is not working normally

neurotoxin (NOOR-oh-*toks*-in) a poison that acts on the brain or the nervous system

paralyzes (PA-ruh-*lize*-iz) causes something to be unable to move

plantations (plan-TAY-shuhnz) large farms where crops such as sugar cane, cotton, or coffee are grown

puffer fish (PUHF-ur FISH) a fish that inflates like a balloon when threatened and contains poisonous body parts

radiation (*ray*-dee-AY-shuhn) a form of energy that can be very dangerous

resurrect (*rez*-uh-REKT) to bring back to life after death

revenants (REV-uh-nahnts) people who have returned from the dead, usually by climbing out of their graves

slavery (SLAY-vuh-ree) forcing people to work for no pay, usually under terrible conditions

tombs (TOOMZ) places where people are buried

toxic (TOK-sik) poisonous, deadly

voodoo (VOO-doo) a religion that includes some traditional African beliefs

witch doctor (WICH *dok*-tur) a priest, magician, or other person with powers to heal and perform religious ceremonies

zombie (ZOM-bee) a dead body that rises out of the grave in a trance

Bibliography

Biology Online: www.biology-online.org/articles/dead_man_walking.html

Bishop, Kyle William. *American Zombie Gothic: The Rise and Fall (and Rise) of the Walking Dead in Popular Culture.* Jefferson, NC: McFarland & Co. (2010).

Morris, Hamilton. "Spirit of the Dead Alive and Well in Haiti." CNN (October 27, 2010). www.cnn.com/2010/WORLD/americas/10/26/vbs.haiti.nzambi/index.html

Read More

Krensky, Stephen. *Zombies (Monster Chronicles).* Minneapolis, MN: Lerner (2008).

Pipe, Jim. *Zombies (Tales of Horror).* New York: Bearport, 2007.

Rooney, Anne. *Zombies on the Loose (Crabtree Contact).* New York: Crabtree (2008).

Learn More Online

To learn more about zombies, visit
www.bearportpublishing.com/NotNearNormal

Index

About the Author

Ruth Owen has been developing, editing, and writing children's books for more than ten years. She lives in Cornwall, England, just minutes from the ocean. Ruth loves gardening and caring for her family of llamas.

J 398.21 OWEN

Owen, Ruth.
Zombies and other
walking dead

SOF

R4002826135

SOUTH FULTON BRANCH
Atlanta-Fulton Public Library